PIANO PIECES
FOR ADULT
BEGINNERS

Compiled and edited by Amy Appleby

This book Copyright © 2000 by Amsco Publications,
A Division of Music Sales Corporation, New York

Order No. AM 967450
US International Standard Book Number: 0.8256.1821.5
UK International Standard Book Number: 0.7119.8501.4

Exclusive Distributors:
Music Sales Corporation
257 Park Avenue South, New York, NY 10010 USA
Music Sales Limited
8/9 Frith Street, London W1D 3JB England
Music Sales Pty. Limited
120 Rothschild Street, Rosebery, Sydney, NSW 2018, Australia

Printed in the United States of America by
Vicks Lithograph and Printing Corporation

Amsco Publications
New York/London/Paris/Sydney/Copenhagen/Madrid/Tokyo/Berlin

PIANO PIECES FOR ADULT BEGINNERS

COMPOSER'S INDEX

POPULAR FAVORITES

FOLK SONGS

PIANO PIECES FOR ADULT BEGINNERS

CONTENTS

Minuet in G

Johann Sebastian Bach
(1685–1750)

Moderately

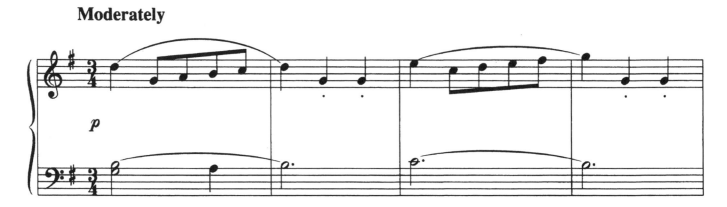

Minuet in D Minor

Johann Sebastian Bach
(1685–1750)

Moderately

Sonata in A
(First Movement)

Wolfgang Amadeus Mozart
(1756–1791)

Andante grazioso

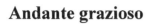

Piano Concerto in E-Flat
(Slow Movement)

Wolfgang Amadeus Mozart
(1756–1791)

Moderately

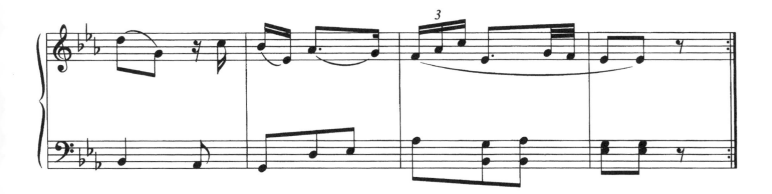

Air

(from *Water Music*)

George Frideric Handel
(1685–1759)

Fairly slow

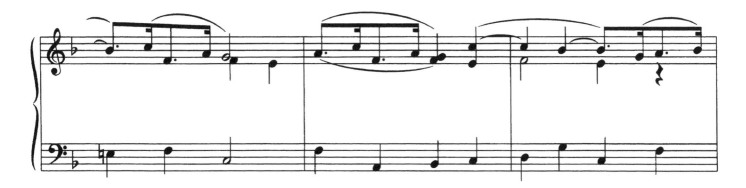

Dance of the Hours

(from *La Gioconda*)

Amilcare Ponchielli
(1834–1886)

Moderately

G7

Trumpet Tune

Henry Purcell
(1659–1695)

With movement

Autumn

(from *The Four Seasons*)

Antonio Vivaldi
(1678–1741)

Allegro

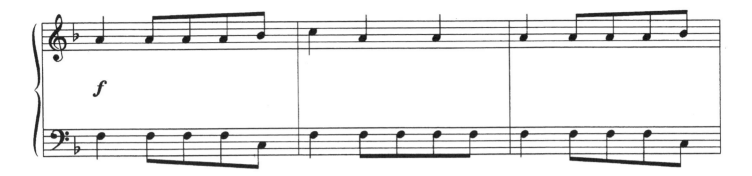

Minuet

(from *String Quintet in E Major, Op. 13, No. 5*)

Luigi Boccherini
(1743–1805)

Moderately

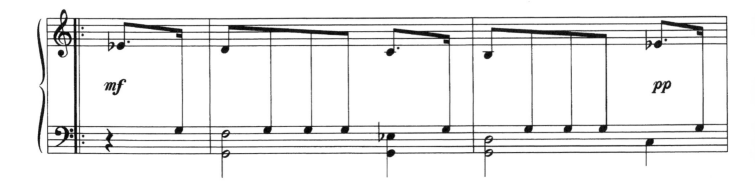

Fine

Pathétique Symphony
(First Movement)

Peter Ilyich Tchaikovsky
(1840–1893)

Theme

(from *Swan Lake*)

Peter Ilyich Tchaikovsky
(1840–1893)

Vive L'Amour

French Folk Song

Lively

When the Saints Come Marchin' In

African-American Folk Song

Spirited walking tempo

Oh, I'm just a wear-y pil-grim,— Trav'-lin' thru this world of sin; Get-tin'

read-y for the day _____ When the saints come march-in' in. _____ Oh, when the

saints _____ come march-in' in, When the saints come march-in' in, Lord, I

want to be in that num-ber,_____ When the saints come march-in' in.

I Love a Piano

Words and music by Irving Berlin

Lively

I love a pian-o,—— I love a pian-o,—— I love to hear some-bod-y

play—— Up-on a pian-o,—— a grand pi-an-o,—— It simp-ly car-ries me a-

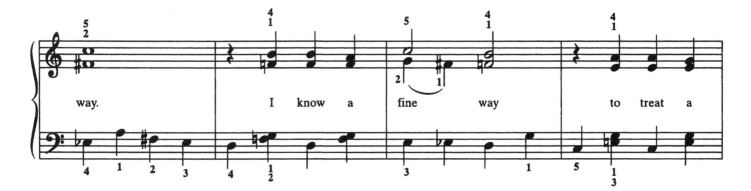

way. I know a fine way to treat a

Stein-way. I love to run my fin-gers o'er the keys,—— the

i - vor - ies.___ And with the ped - al_____ I love to med - dle._____ When Pa - de -

rew - ski comes this way,_____ I'm so de - light - ed,_____ If I'm in -

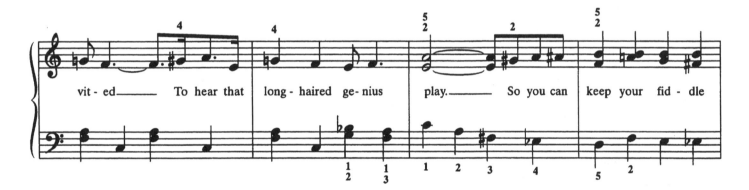

vit - ed_____ To hear that long - haired ge - nius play.____ So you can keep your fid - dle

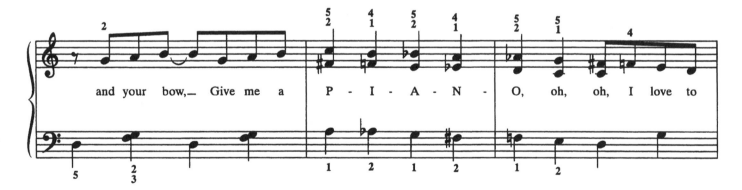

and your bow,__ Give me a P - I - A - N - O, oh, oh, I love to

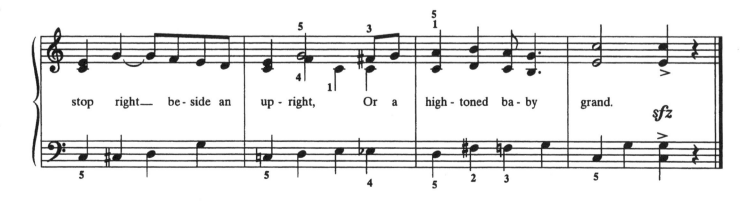

stop right__ be - side an up - right, Or a high - toned ba - by grand.

Marche Militaire

Franz Schubert
(1797–1828)

Allegro moderato

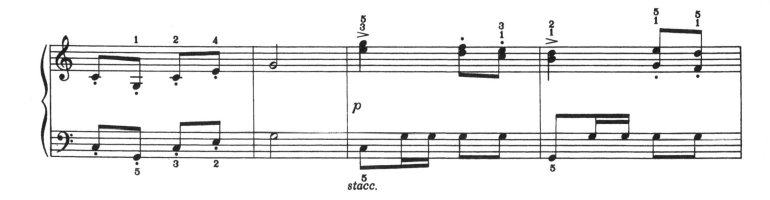

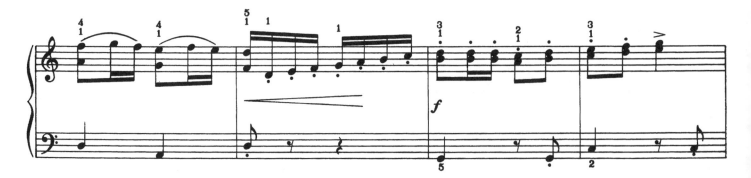

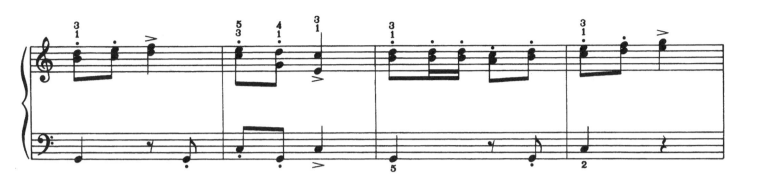

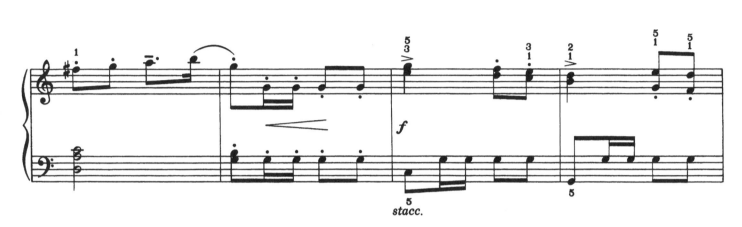

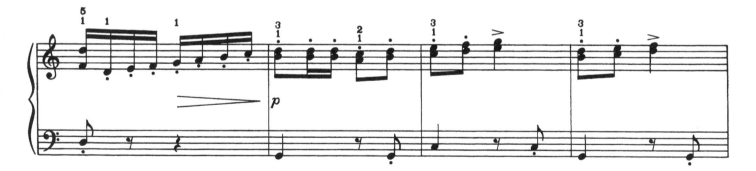

Piano Concerto No. 4
(First Movement)

Ludwig van Beethoven
(1770–1827)

Allegro moderato

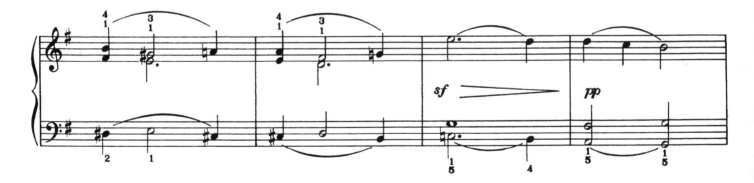

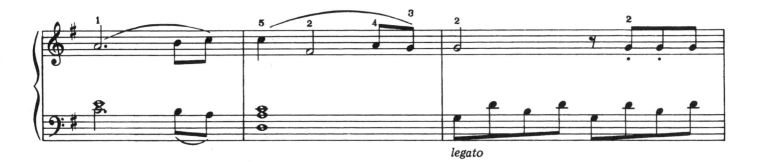

legato

dim.

pp

Aura Lee

Words by W.W. Fosdick

Simply, tenderly

As the black-bird in the spring 'Neath the wil-low tree____

Sat and piped, I heard him sing, Sing of Au - ra Lee.

Chorus

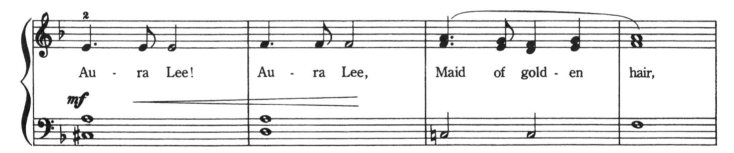

Au - ra Lee! Au - ra Lee, Maid of gold - en hair,

Sun - shine came a - long with thee, and swal - lows in the air.

I Love You Truly

Carrie Jacobs-Bond

Rather slow

1. I love you tru - ly, tru - ly dear,
2. Ah! love, 'tis some - thing to feel your kind hand,

Life with its sor - row, life with its tear,
Ah! yes, 'tis some - thing by your side to stand;

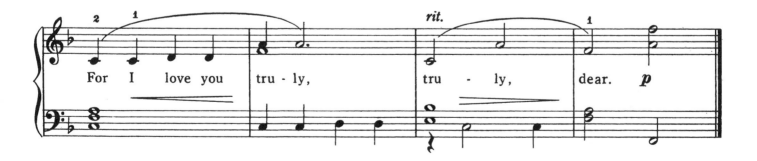

Fades in - to dreams when I feel you are near,
Gone is the sor - row, gone doubt and fear,

For I love you tru - ly, tru - ly, dear.

Sonata for Violin and Piano

(Last Movement)

Wolfgang Amadeus Mozart
(1756–1791)

With movement

Morning

(from *Peer Gynt*)

Edvard Grieg
(1843–1907)

Not too fast

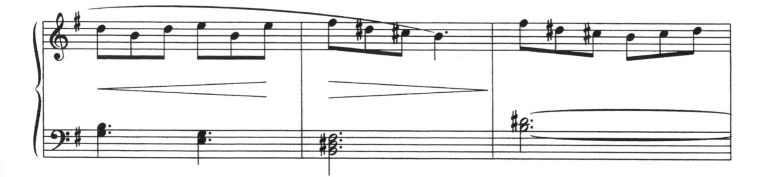

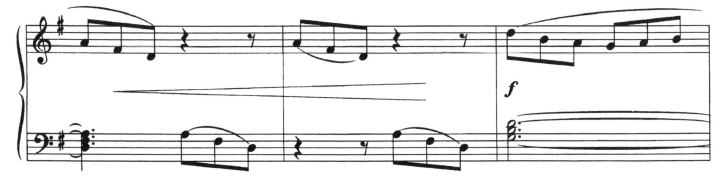

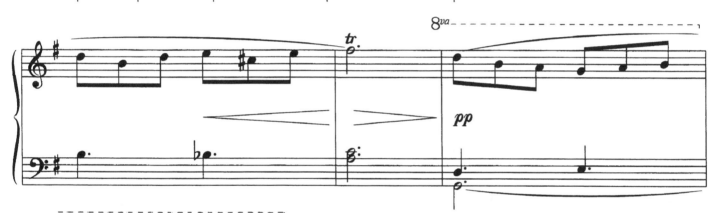

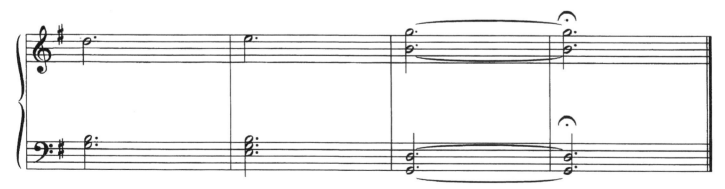

Wedding Marches

Richard Wagner
(1813–1883)

Felix Mendelssohn
(1809–1847)

Andante

After You've Gone

Words and music by
Henry Creamer & Turner Layton

There'll come a time,— now don't for-get it, There'll come a time—

when you'll re-gret it. Some day, when you grow lone — ly,

Your heart will break like mine and you'll went me on - .ly, Af-ter you've gone,—

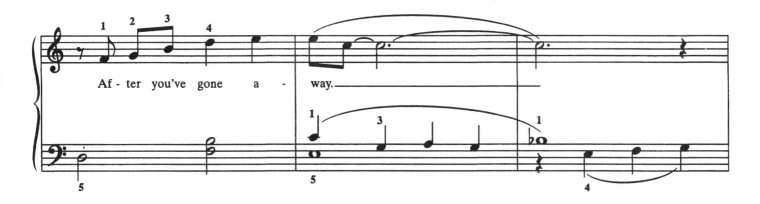

Af-ter you've gone a - way.

Sally in Our Alley

English Folk Song

1. Of all the girls____ that are so smart,____ There's none like pret-ty
2. Of all the days____ that's in the week,____ I dear - ly love but
3. My mas-ter and____ the neigh-bours all,____ Make game of me and

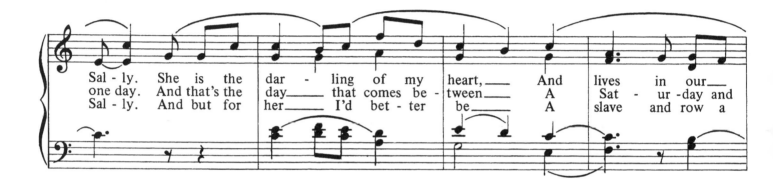

Sal - ly. She is the dar - ling of my heart,____ And lives in our____
one day. And that's the day____ that comes be - tween____ A Sat - ur -day and
Sal - ly. And but for her____ I'd bet - ter be____ A slave and row a

al - ley. There is no la - dy in the land That's half so sweet as____
Mon-day. For then I'm dressed in all my best, To walk a - broad with____
gal - ley. But when my seven long years are out, Oh then I'll mar - ry____

Sal - ly;
Sal - ly; } She is the dar - ling of my heart____ And she lives in our____ al-ley.
Sal - ly;

The Minstrel Boy

Irish Folk Song

Minuet

Wolfgang Amadeus Mozart
(1756–1791)

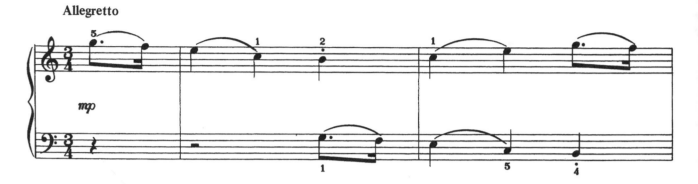

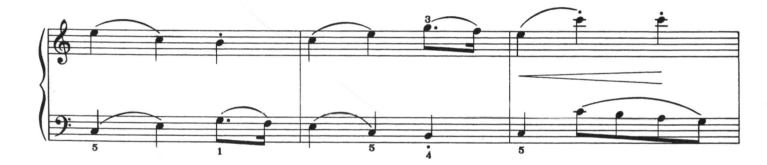

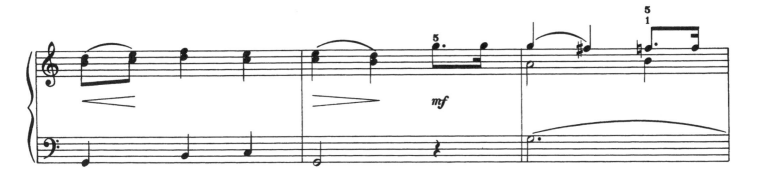

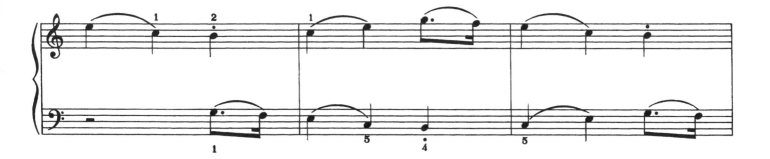

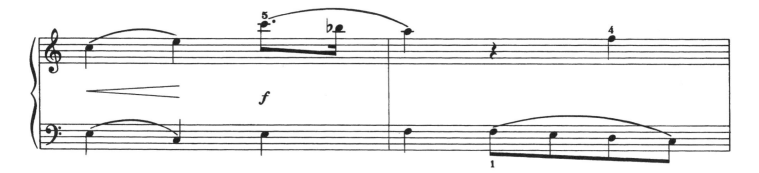

poco rit.

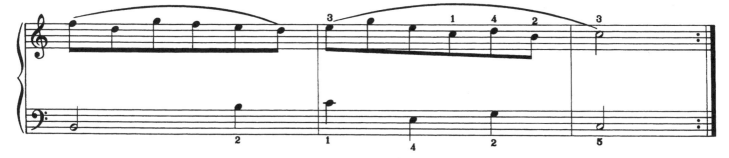

Partita No. 1
(Second Minuet)

Johann Sebastian Bach
(1685–1750)

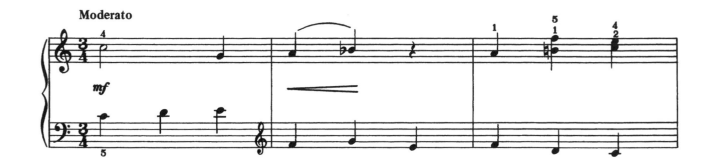

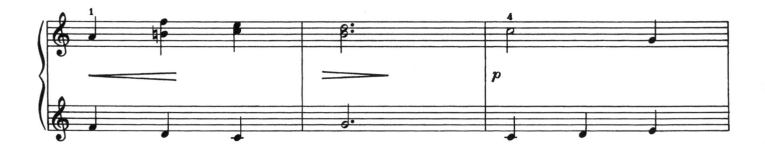

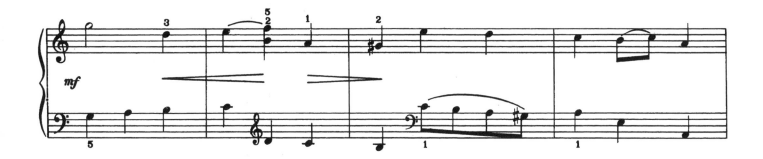

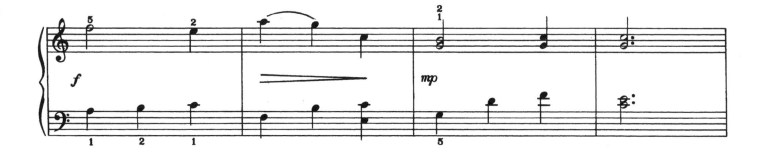

poco rit. - - - - - - - - - - - - - - -

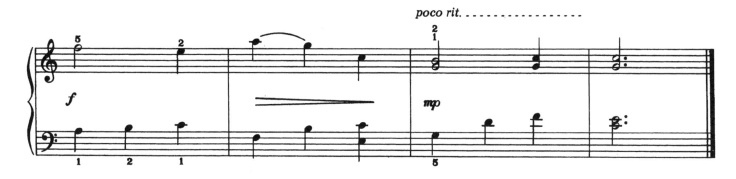

Liebestraum

Franz Liszt
(1811–1886)

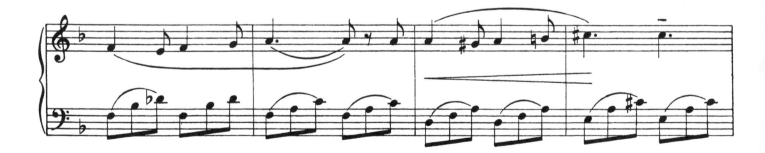

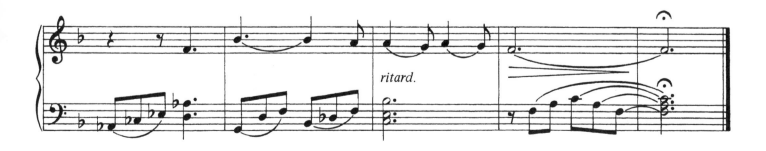

Ah! So Pure

(from *Martha*)

Friedrich von Flotow
(1812–1883)

Moderato

with Pedal

Symphony No. 6
(Canto Pastoral)

Ludwig van Beethoven
(1770–1827)

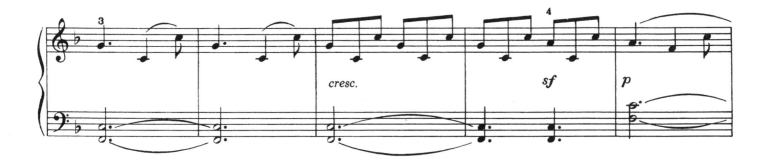

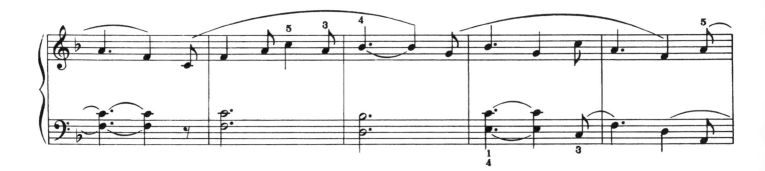

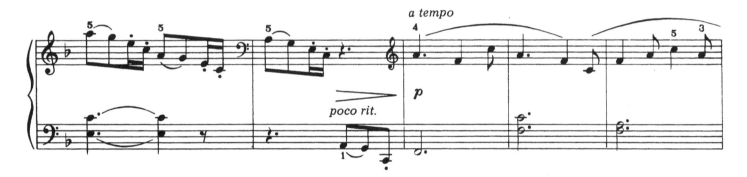

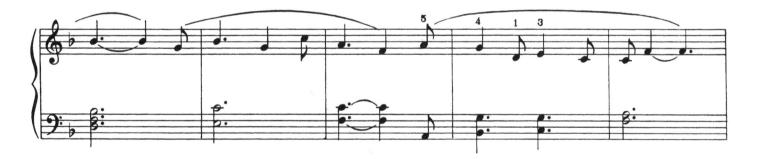

Prelude
(Op. 28, No. 4)

Frédéric Chopin
(1810–1849)

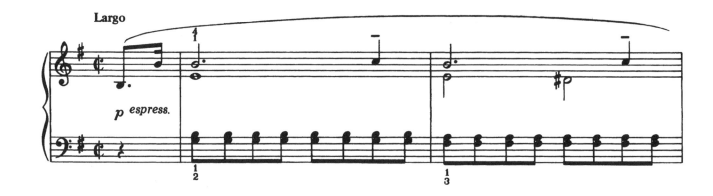

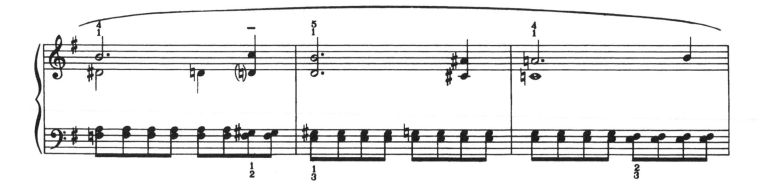

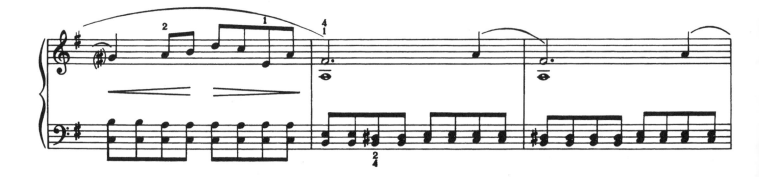

Etude
(Op. 10, No. 3)

Frédéric Chopin
(1810–1849)

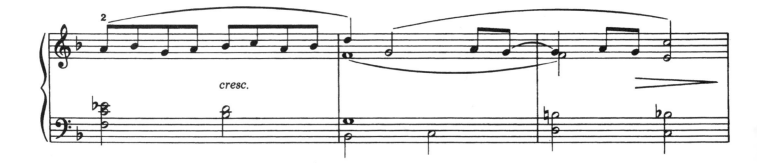

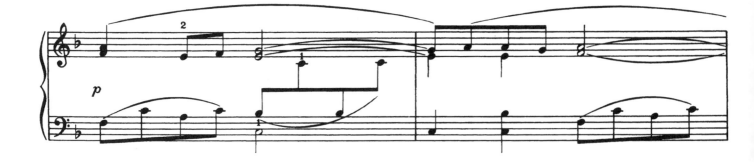

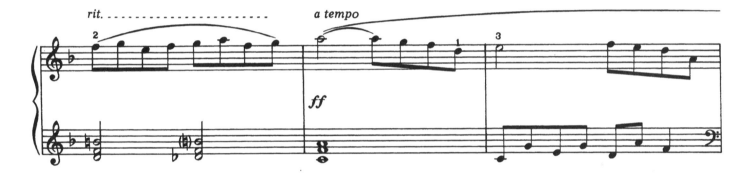

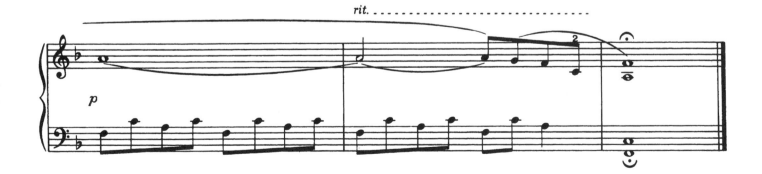

In Stilly Night

German Folk Song

Peacefully

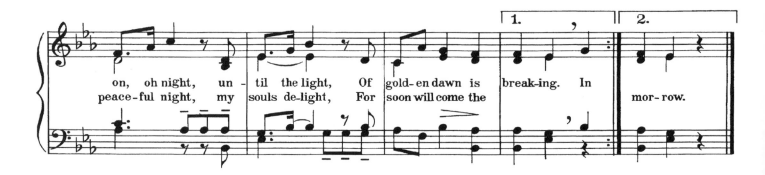

Stodola Pumpa

Czech Folk Dance

Bright tempo

Sto-do-la, sto-do-la, sto-do-la pum-pa, Sto-do-la pum-pa, sto-do-la pum-pa,

f - p

2. *Fine* **Slower**

pum, pum, pum. Hey! Walk - ing a - long with my dear maid - en gay,
Out of the wood the night - in - gale's sweet song,

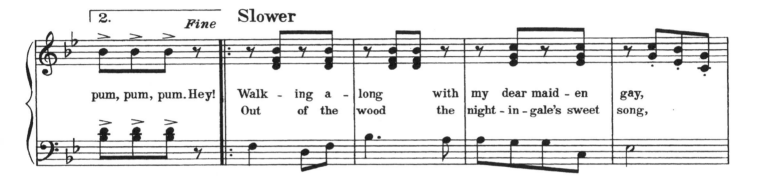

Stars shin-ing bright to light our mer - ry way. Walk - ing a - long with
Told my dear maid - en of my love so strong. Out of the wood the

my dear maid-en gay, Stars shin-ing bright to light our mer - ry way. Hey!
night-in-gale's sweet song, Told my dear maid - en of my love so strong. Hey!

D. C. al Fine

Solveig's Song

Edvard Grieg
(1843–1907)

Fingal's Cave

Felix Mendelssohn
(1809–1847)

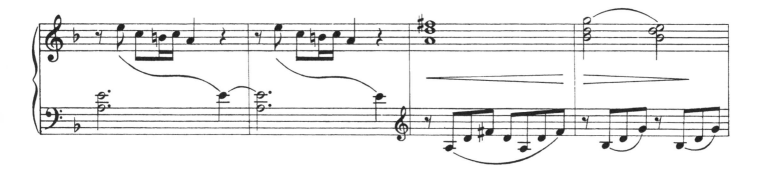

Ave Maria

Franz Schubert
(1797–1828)

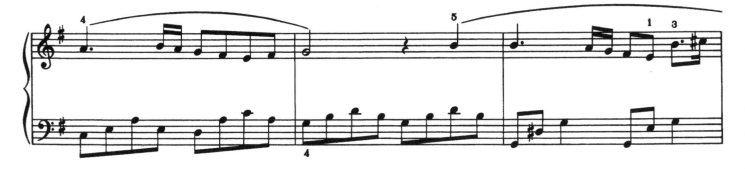

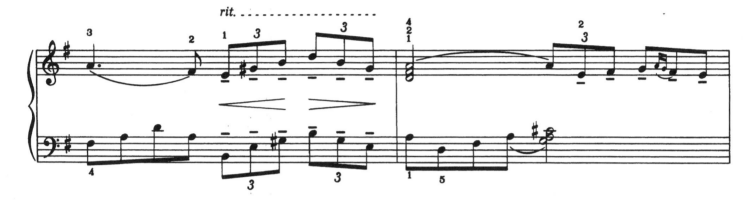

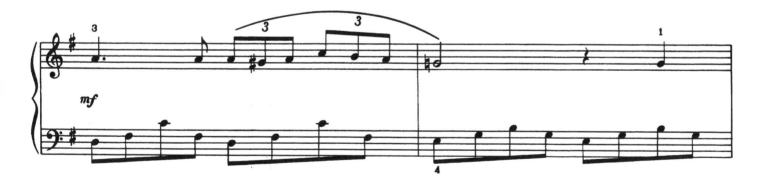

Death and the Maiden

Franz Schubert
(1797–1828)

Liberty Bell

John Philip Sousa
(1854-1932)

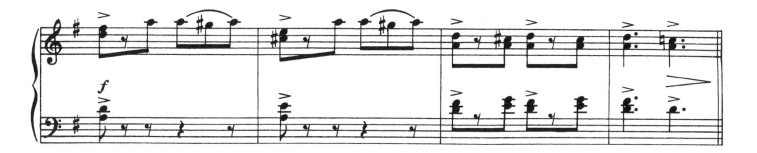

D.S. al Fine

Havah Nagilah

Israeli Hora

Fine

Ha - vah_____ na - gi - lah, Sing! Let us re - joice!

Ha - vah n' - ra - ne - nah, Ha - vah n' - ra - ne - nah,

Ha - vah n' - ra - ne - nah, Sing! Let us re - joice!

Ha - vah n' - ra - ne - nah, Ha - vah n' - ra - ne - nah,

Wake with a hap - py heart, Sing! Let us re - joice!

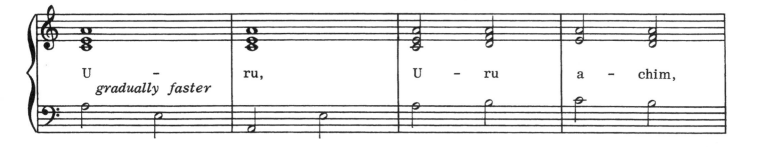

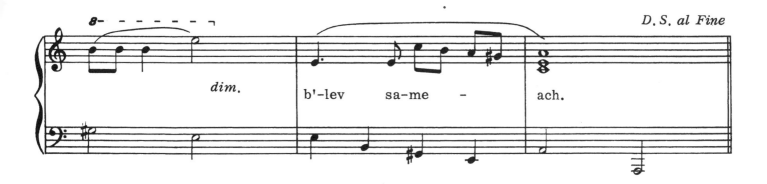

Danube Waves
(Anniversary Waltz)

Iosif Ivanovici
(c. 1845–1902)

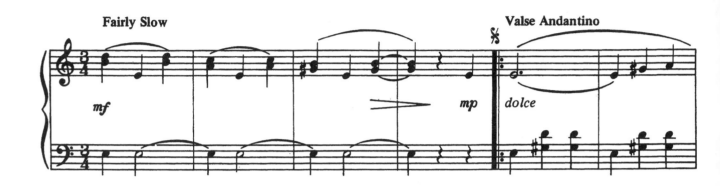

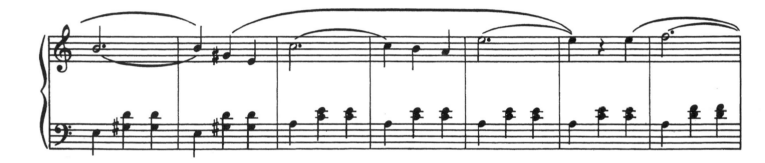

poco rit   a tempo

ritard.   D.S. al fine

Ciribiribin

A. Pestalozza

Valse

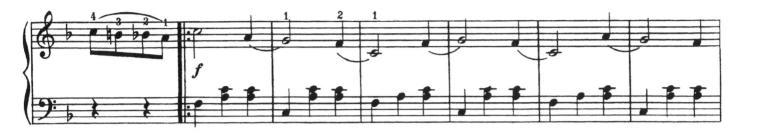

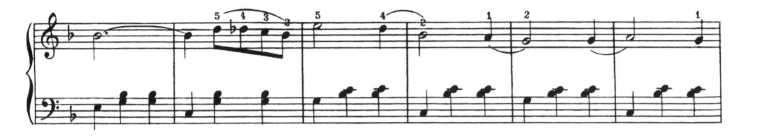

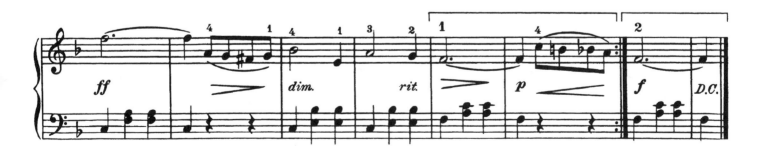

Serenade for Strings
(Waltz)

Peter Ilyich Tchaikovsky
(1840–1893)

In the Good Old Summer Time

Words by Ren Shields

Music by George Evans

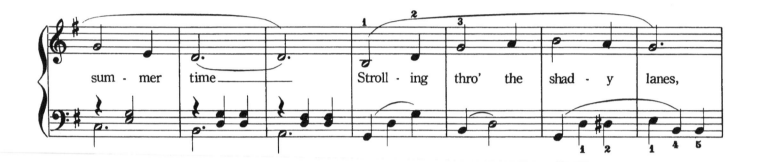

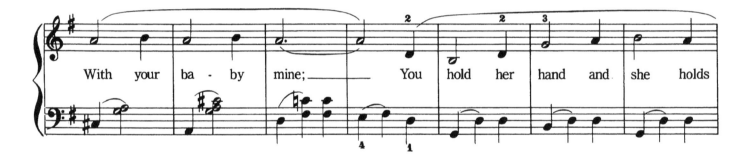

The Sidewalks of New York

Words and music by
James W. Blake & Charles B. Lawlor

Lively waltz

East side, West side, All a-round the town,

The tots sang "ring a ro-sie," "Lon - don Bridge is fall - ing

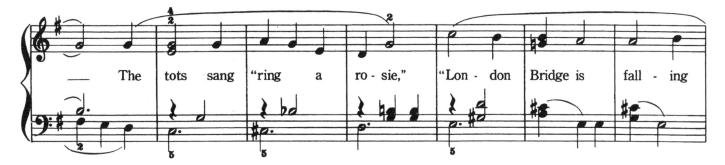

down." Boys and girls to - geth - er,

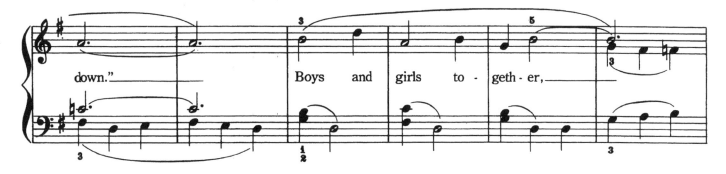

Me and Ma - mie O' Rorke, We tripped the light fan -

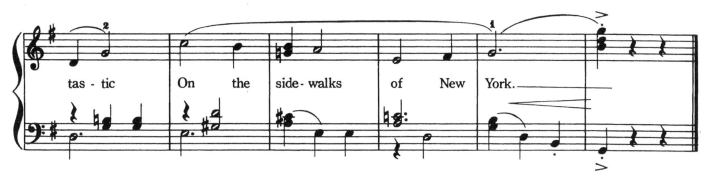

tas - tic On the side - walks of New York.

Meet Me in St. Louis

Words and music by Kerry Mills

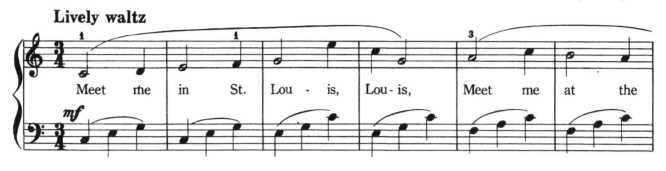

Meet me in St. Lou - is, Lou - is, Meet me at the

fair,_____ Don't tell me the lights are shin - ing

An - y - place but there;_____ We will dance the Hooch - ee Koo - chee,_____

_____ I will be your toots - ie woots - ie, If you will meet me

in St. Lou - is, Lou - is, Meet me at the fair._____

Give My Regards to Broadway

Words and music by George M. Cohan

Give my re-gards to Broad - way, Re-mem-ber me to Her - ald

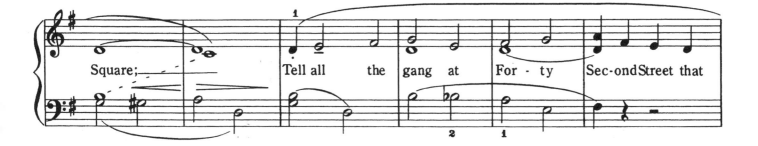

Square;____ Tell all the gang at For - ty Sec-ond Street that

I will soon be there.____ Whis-per of how I'm yearn -

ing to min-gle with the old time throng;____ Give my re-gards to

old Broad - way and say that I'll be there, e'er long.____

Skaters Waltz

Emil Waldteufel
(1837–1915)

D.S. al fine

I Have a Song to Sing-O

(from The Yeomen of the Guard)

Words by William S. Gilbert
(1836–1911)

Music by Arthur Sullivan
(1842–1900)

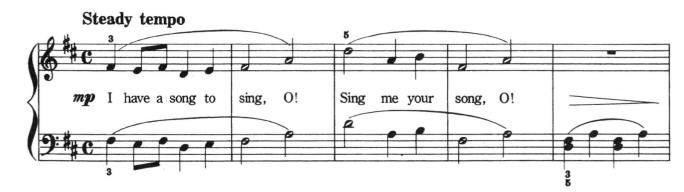

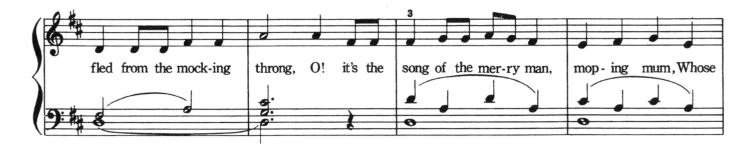

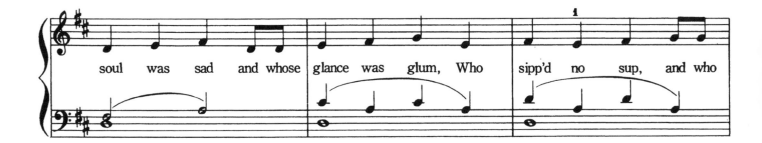

Heigh - dy! Heigh - dy! Mis-er-y me, Lack-a-day-dee! He

sipp'd no sup, and he crav'd no crumb, As he sigh'd for the love of a la - dye!

The Flowers That Bloom in the Spring

(from *The Mikado*)

Words by William S. Gilbert
(1836–1911)

Music by Arthur Sullivan
(1842–1900)

Gaily

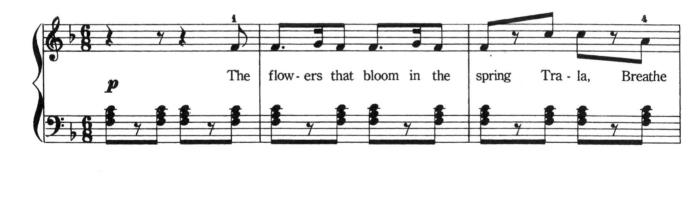

The flow-ers that bloom in the spring Tra - la, Breathe

prom-ise of mer-ry sun - shine;___ As we mer-ri-ly dance and we sing Tra-la, We

The Band Played On

Words by John F. Palmer

Music by Charles B. Ward

Bill Bailey

Bright cake-walk

Words and music by Hughie Cannon

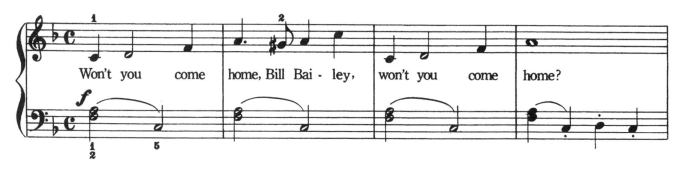

Won't you come home, Bill Bai - ley, won't you come home?

She moans the whole day long; _____ I'll do the

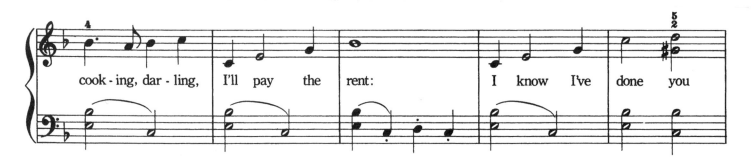

cook - ing, dar - ling, I'll pay the rent: I know I've done you

wrong. _____ 'Mem - ber that rain - y eve - ning I drove you

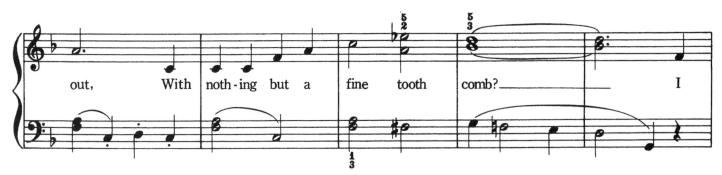

out, With noth - ing but a fine tooth comb? _____ I

know I'm to blame; well ain't that a shame? Bill

Bai - ley won't you please come home?

I Dream of Jeanie with the Light Brown Hair

Words and music by Stephen Foster

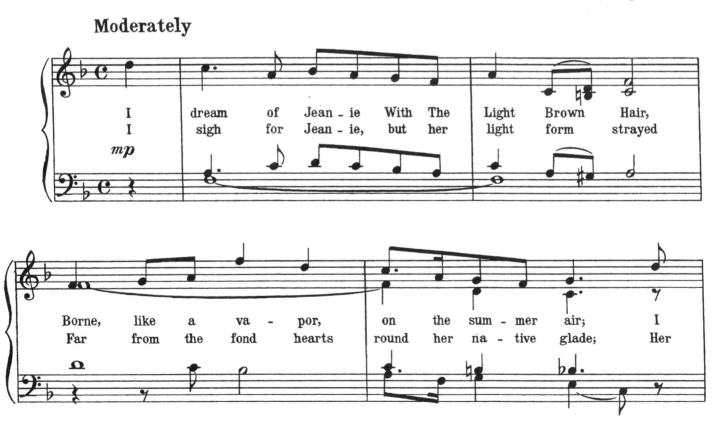

Moderately

mp

I dream of Jean - ie With The Light Brown Hair,
I sigh for Jean - ie, but her light light form strayed

Borne, like a va - por, on the sum - mer air; I
Far from the fond hearts round her na - tive glade; Her

see her trip-ping where the bright streams play,
smiles have van-ished and her sweet songs flown,

Hap-py as the dai - sies that
Flit-ting like the dreams that have

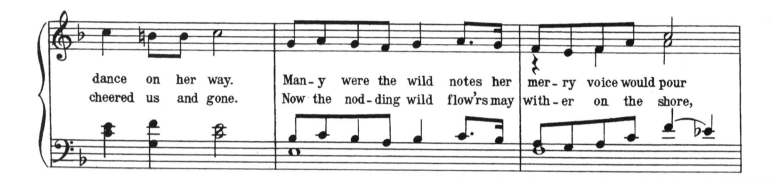

dance on her way. Man-y were the wild notes her mer-ry voice would pour
cheered us and gone. Now the nod-ding wild flow'rs may with-er on the shore,

Man-y were the blithe birds that war - bled them o'er: I dream of Jean-ie With The
While her gen-tle fin - gers will cull them no more; I sigh for Jean-ie With The

Light Brown Hair, Float-ing like a va-por on the soft, sum-mer air.
Light Brown Hair, Float-ing like a va-por on the soft, sum-mer air.

Auld Lang Syne

Words by Robert Burns

Scottish Air

Funeral March of a Marionette

Charles Gounod
(1818–1893)

Allegretto

William Tell Overture

Gioacchino Rossini
(1792–1868)

Moderato

Can Can

(from Orpheus in the Underworld)

Jacques Offenbach
(1819–1880)

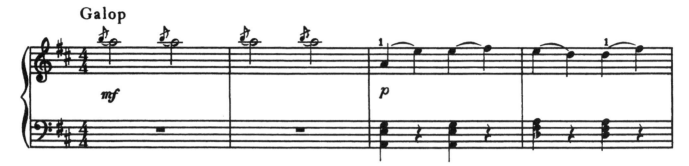

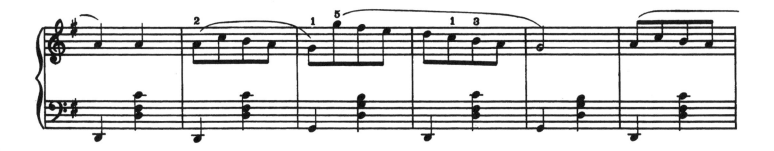

Waltz
(from *Sleeping Beauty*)

Peter Ilyich Tchaikovsky
(1840–1893)

Valse Moderato

Fine

D.C. al fine

Pathétique Sonata
(Adagio)

Ludwig van Beethoven
(1770–1827)

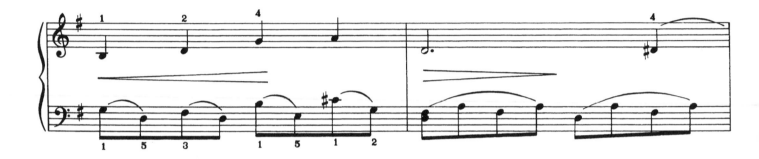

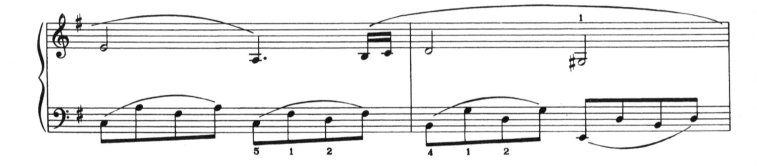

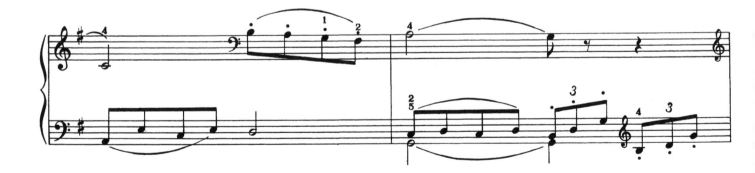

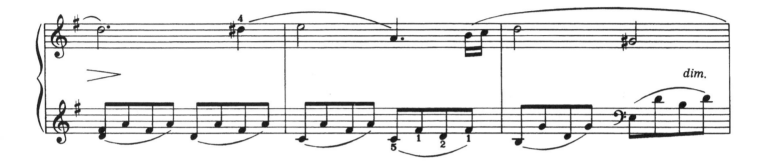

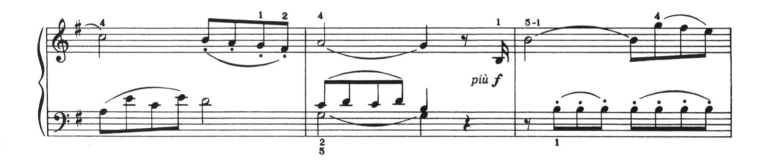

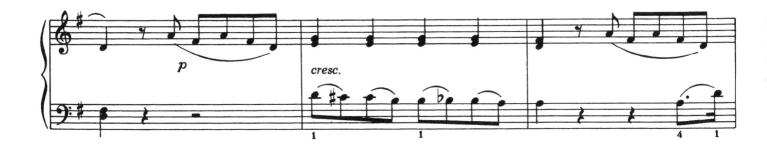

Nocturne
(Op. 9, No. 2)

Frédéric Chopin
(1810–1849)

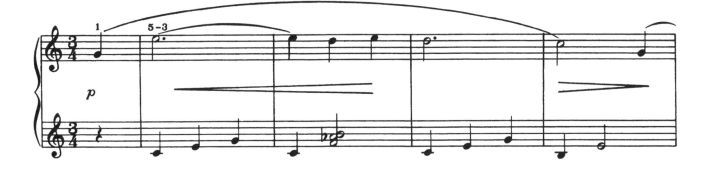

Look for the Silver Lining

Words and music by Jerome Kern

Moderately slow, with expression

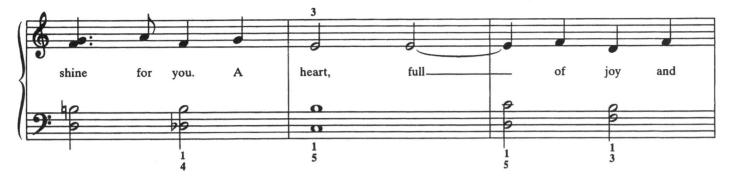

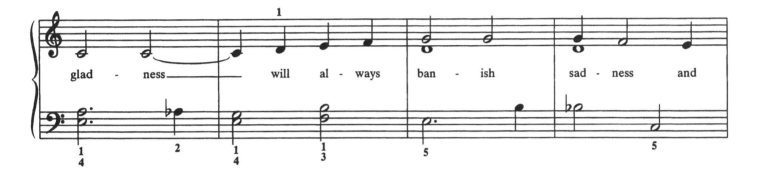

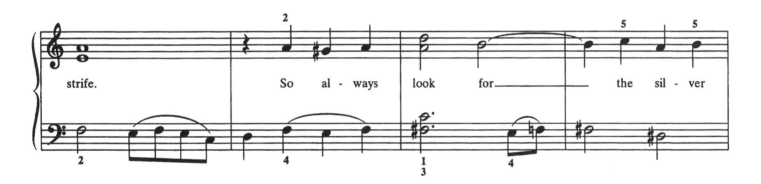

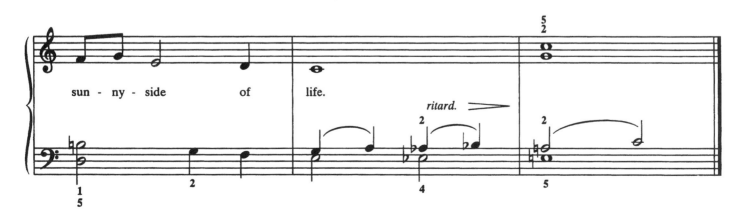

Prelude No. 9

Johann Sebastian Bach
(1685–1750)

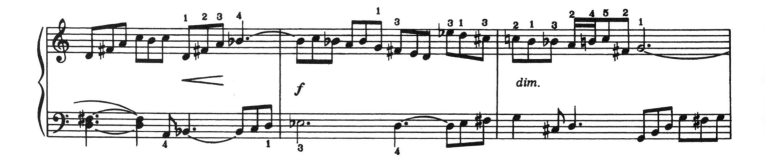

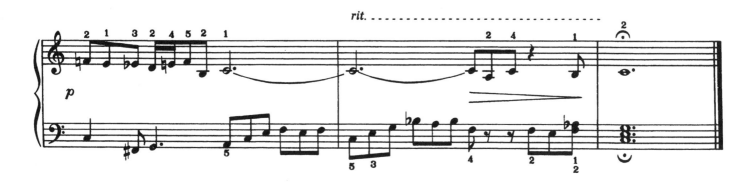

Air on the G String

Johann Sebastian Bach
(1685–1750)

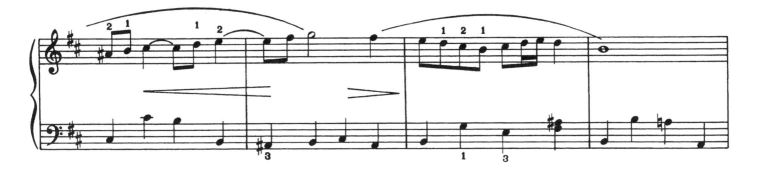

Jesu, Joy of Man's Desiring

Johann Sebastian Bach
(1685–1750)

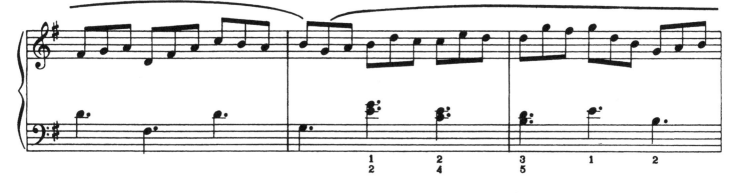

Hungarian Dance No.6

Johannes Brahms
(1833–1897)

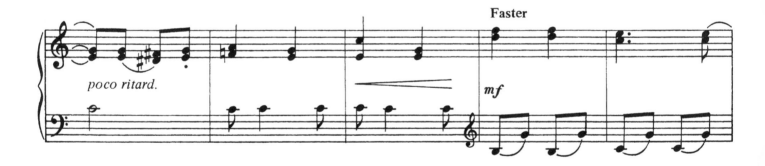

Tempo primo

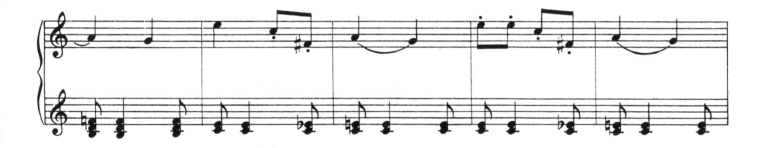

Romance

(from *Eine Kleine Nachtmusik*)

Wolfgang Amadeus Mozart
(1756–1791)

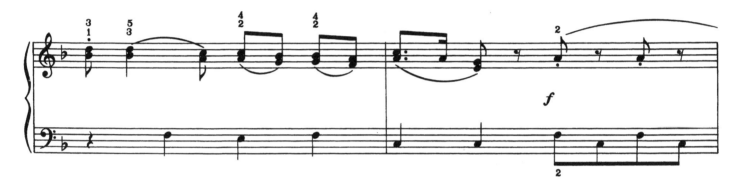

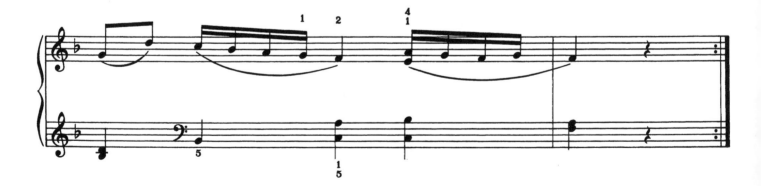

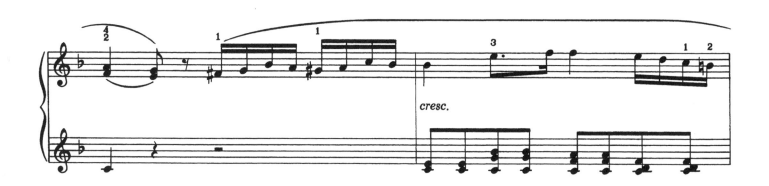

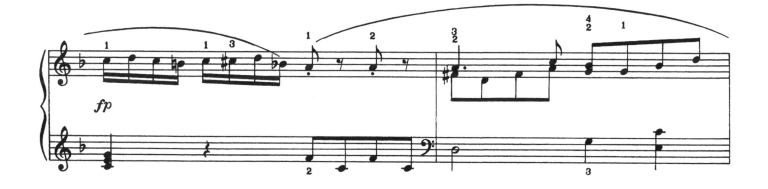

Rondo

(from *Eine Kleine Nachtmusik*)

Wolfgang Amadeus Mozart
(1756–1791)

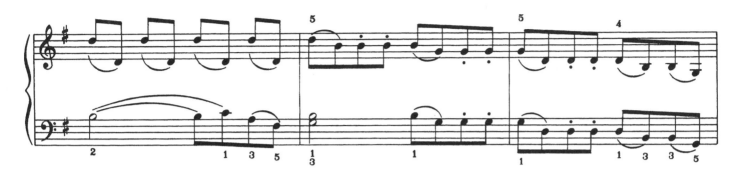

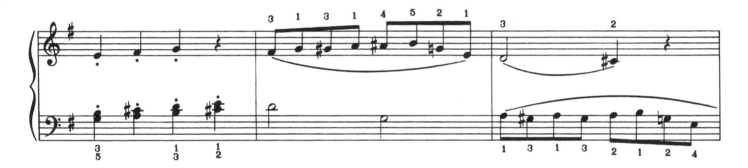

Tales from the Vienna Woods

Johann Strauss
(1825–1899)

Moderate

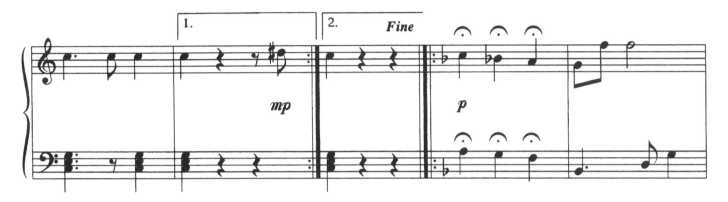

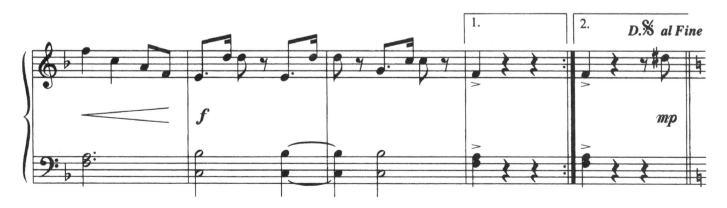

Slumber Song

Robert Schumann
(1810–1856)

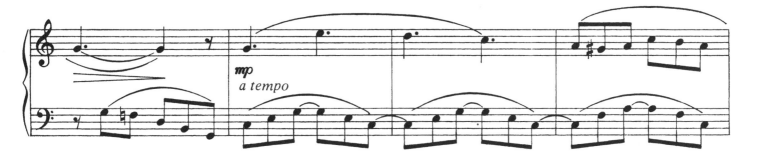

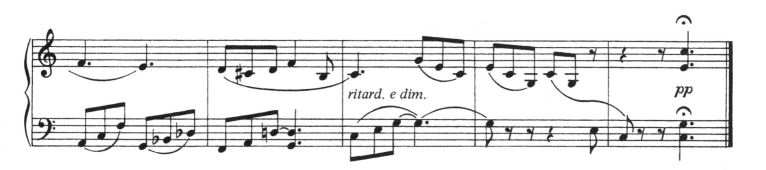

Symphony No. 40
(Theme)

Wolfgang Amadeus Mozart
(1756–1791)

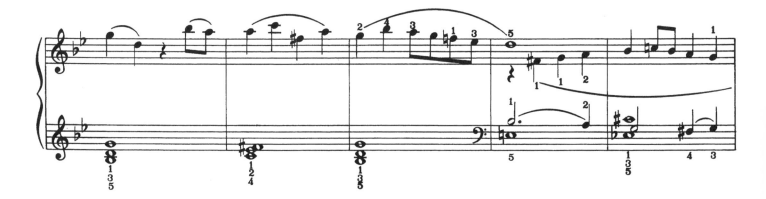

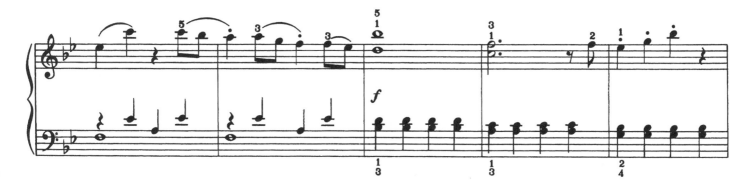

Romance in F

Ludwig van Beethoven
(1770–1827)

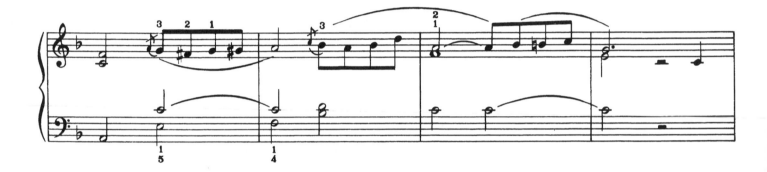

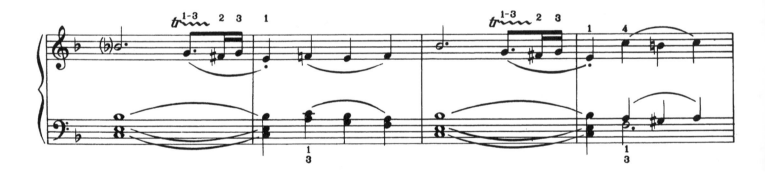

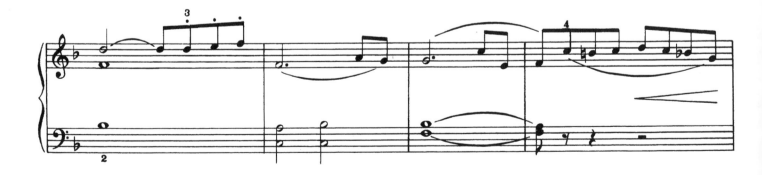

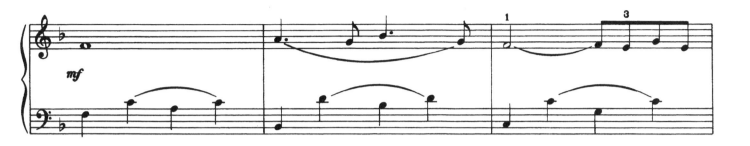

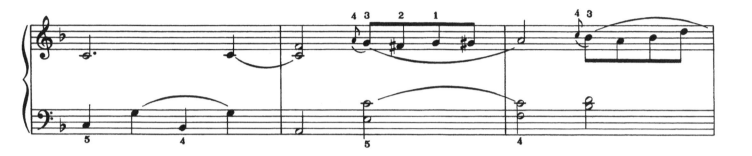

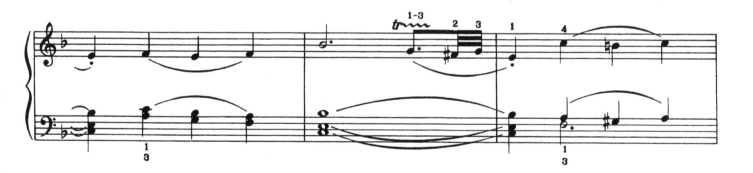

Symphony No. 7
(Theme)

Ludwig van Beethoven
(1770–1827)

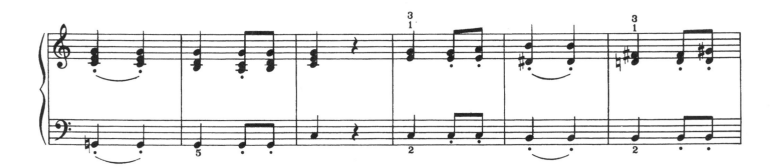

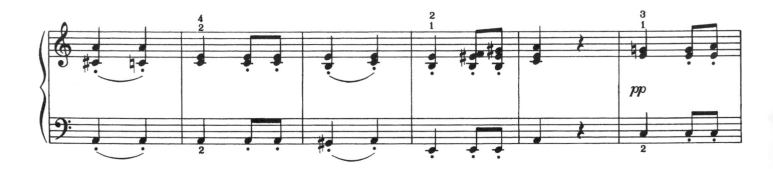

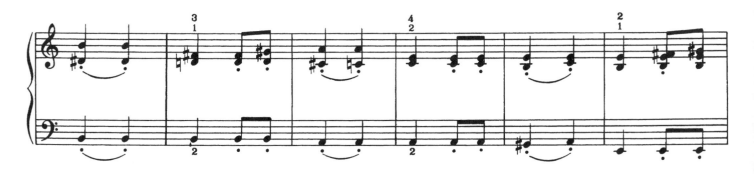

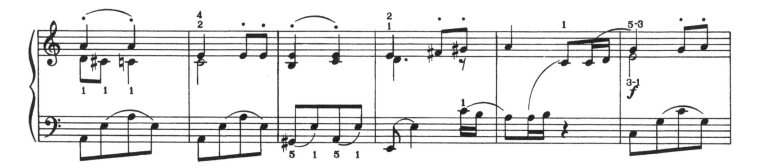

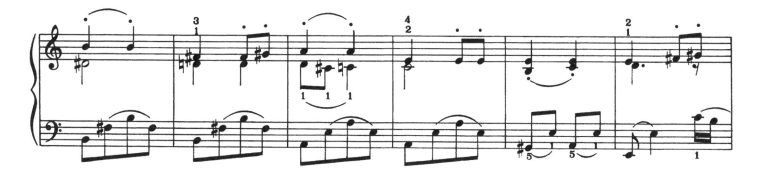

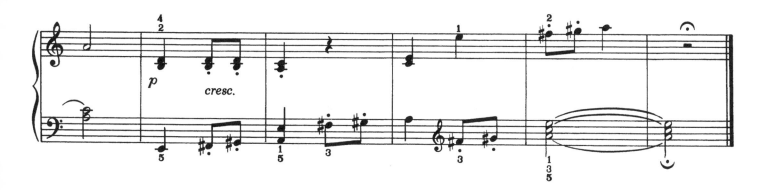

The Kerry Dance

Irish Folk Dance

O the days of the Ker-ry danc-ing, O the ring of the

pi-per's tune! O for one of those hours of glad-ness, Gone a-las like our youth, too soon.

Fine

When the boys be-gan to gath-er in the glen, of a sum-mer night,

And the Ker-ry pi-per's tun-ing made us long _ with wild de-light;

O to think of it, O to dream of it, Fills my heart with tears!

D.S. al Fine

There Is a Tavern in the Town

English Folk Song

Bright polka tempo

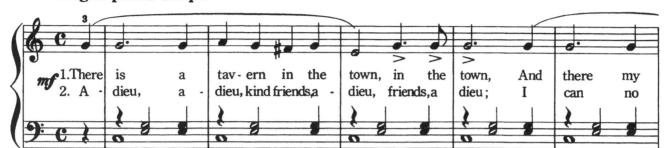

1.There is a tav - ern in the town, in the town, And there my
2. A - dieu, a - dieu, kind friends, a - dieu, friends, a - dieu; I can no

dear love sits him down, sits him down___ And___ drinks his wine 'mid
long - er stay with you, stay with you;___ I'll___ hang my harp on a

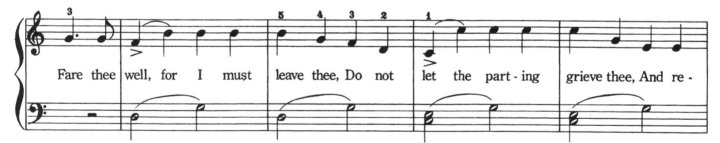

laugh - ter___ free, And nev - er, nev - er thinks of me. *f*
weep-ing wil - low tree, And may the world go well with thee.   *Fine*

Fare thee well, for I must leave thee, Do not let the part - ing grieve thee, And re -

mem - ber that the best of friends must part, must part.

D. C. al Fine

You Made Me Love You

Words by Joseph McCarthy

Music by James V. Monaco

times, dear, you made me feel— so bad. You made me

sigh for, I did-n't want to tell you, I did-n't want to tell you. I want some

love that's true, Yes I do, 'Deed I do, You know I do! Give me, give me

what I cry— for, You know you got the brand of kiss - es that I'd die— for.

You know you made me love you.— sfz

Madame Butterfly
(Themes)

Giacomo Puccini
(1858–1924)

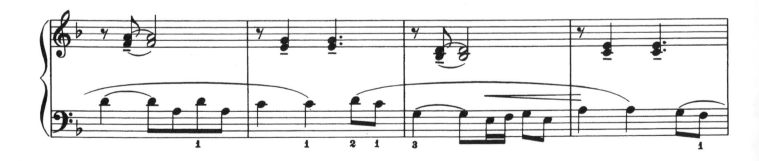

March

(from *The Nutcracker*)

Peter Ilyich Tchaikovsky
(1840–1893)

Anvil Chorus

(from *Il Trovatore*)

Giuseppe Verdi
(1813–1901)

Evening Star

(from *Tannhäuser*)

Richard Wagner
(1813–1883)

Andante moderato

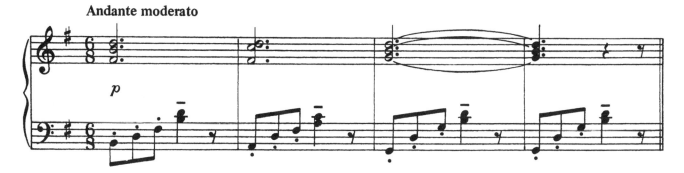

Poco rit.   *a tempo*

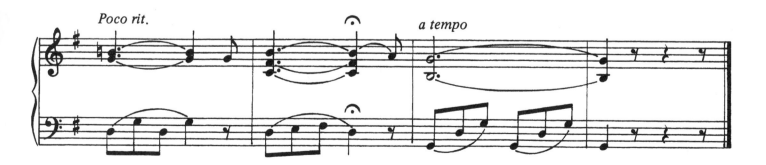

German Dance

Franz Joseph Haydn
(1732–1809)

Trio

D. C. al Fine

I Love You

Edvard Grieg
(1843–1907)

Emperor Waltz

Johann Strauss
(1825–1899)

The Whistler and His Dog

Arthur Pryor

Moderate walking tempo

D.C. al Fine

Aloha Oe

Queen Lydia Liliuokanani

Habanera

(from *Carmen*)

Georges Bizet
(1838–1875)

Hallelujah Chorus
(Themes)

George Frideric Handel
(1685–1759)

Bright tempo

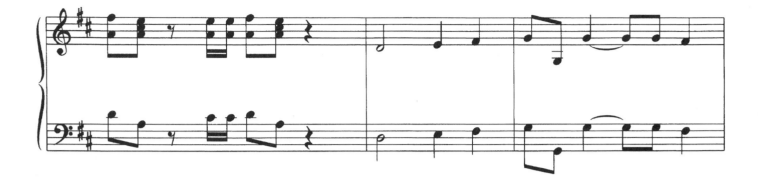

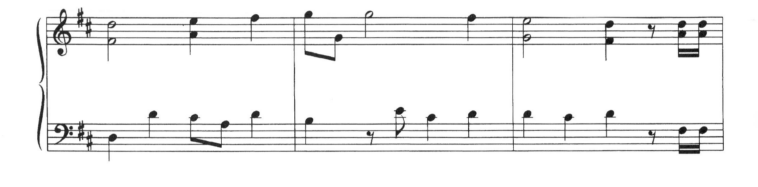

La Cinquantaine
(The Golden Wedding)

Gabriel-Marie
(1852–1920)

Andantino

p

with Pedal

My Wild Irish Rose

Words and music by Chauncey Olcott

My wild I - rish rose, The sweet - est flow'r that

grows, You may search ev - 'ry - where, but none can com - pare With my

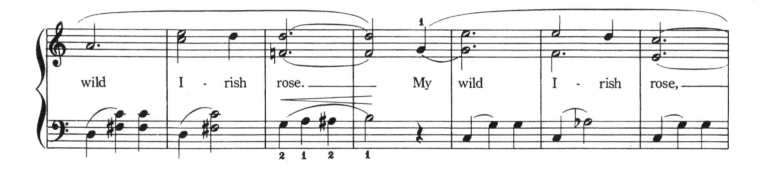

wild I - rish rose. My wild I - rish rose,

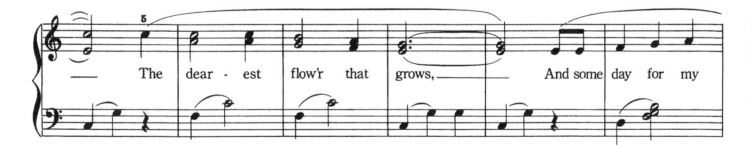

The dear - est flow'r that grows, And some day for my

sake, she may let me take The bloom from my wild I - rish rose.

Down South

W.H. Myddleton

Bright, strutting tempo

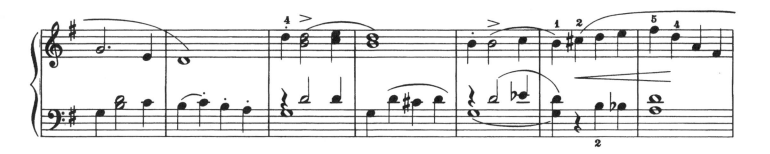

Pizzicati
(from *Sylvia*)

Léo Delibes
(1836–1891)

The Swan

(from *Carnival of the Animals*)

Camille Saint-Saëns
(1835–1921)

Adagio e legato

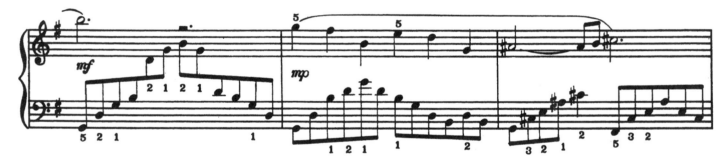

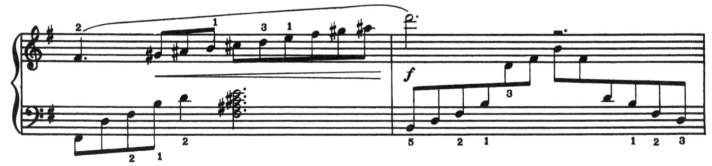

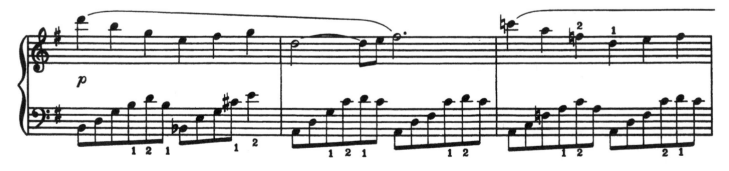

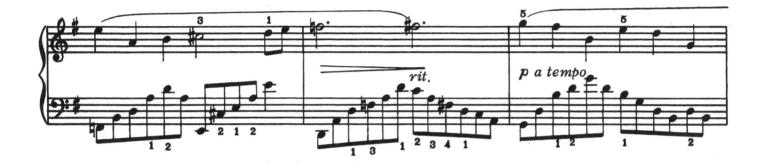

Flight of the Bumble Bee

Nikolai Rimsky-Korsakov
(1844–1908)

Allegro

(from *Suite No. 7*)

George Frideric Handel
(1685–1759)

June

(Barcarolle)

Peter Ilyich Tchaikovsky
(1840–1893)

Polonaise

Frédéric Chopin
(1810–1849)

Moderato

Two-Part Invention No. 1

Johann Sebastian Bach
(1685–1750)

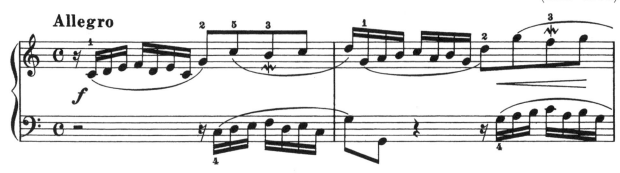

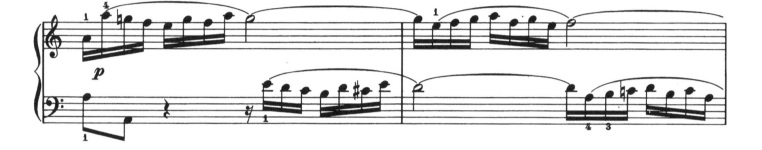

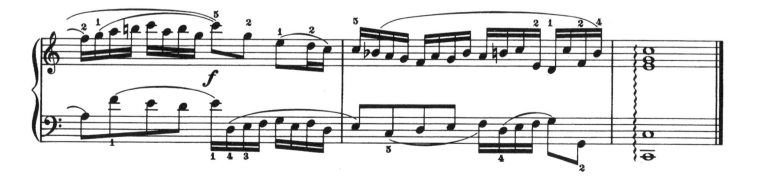

Two-Part Invention No. 3

Johann Sebastian Bach
(1685–1750)

Allegretto

Gavotte

(from *Sixth Cello Suite*)

Johann Sebastian Bach
(1685–1750)

Allegro moderato

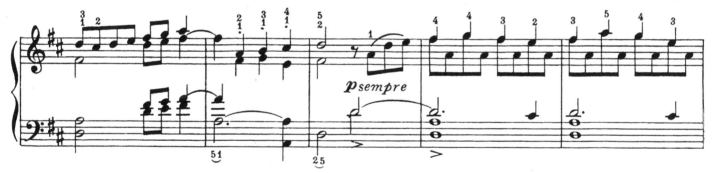

D.C. al Fine
senza ripetizione

Sonata in G

Ludwig van Beethoven
(1770–1827)

Allegro, ma non troppo

Sonata in C

Wolfgang Amadeus Mozart
(1756–1791)

Allegro

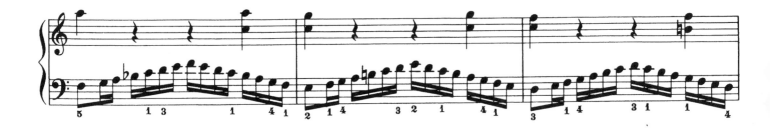

Moonlight Sonata
(Adagio)

Ludwig van Beethoven
(1770–1827)

Adagio sostenuto

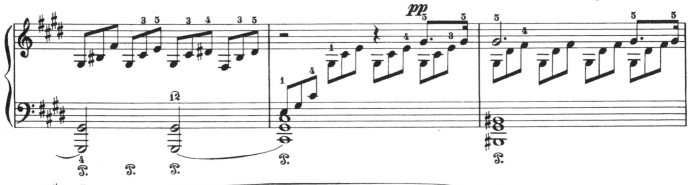

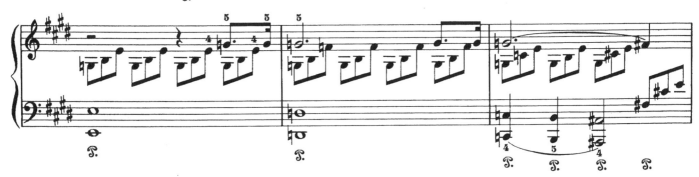

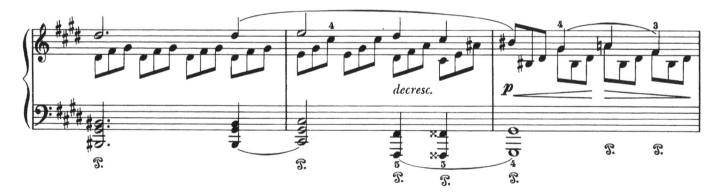

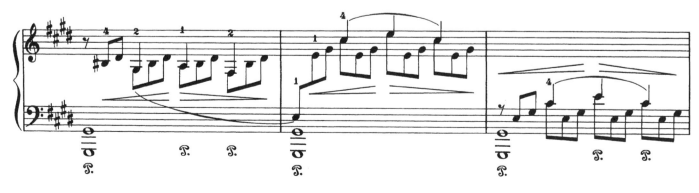

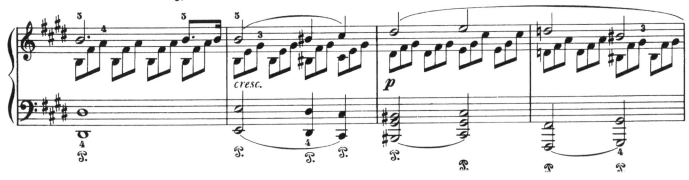

attacca subito il sequento ✻

Maple Leaf Rag

Scott Joplin
(1868–1917)

Lively

D.C. al Fine

GLOSSARY OF MUSIC SYMBOLS

ACCENTS AND ARTICULATIONS

Accent Marks

fz or **ffz** **Forzando.** A strong, loud accent.

fp **Forte piano.** A strong, loud accent which instantly diminishes to a soft volume.

sf, sz, or **sfz** **Sforzando** (also **Sforzato**). A very strong, sudden, and loud accent.

sfp **Sforzando piano.** A very strong, sudden, and loud accent which instantly diminishes to a soft volume

Notes marked with any of these accent signs are to be played with a strong accent and held for their full note value.

Slurs

A curved line connecting two or more notes indicates that they should be played smoothly.

Sometimes a slur is used with staccato markings to indicate that the notes be played halfway between staccato and legato—detached, yet somewhat smooth.

Staccato Marks

A dot above or below a note or chord indicates that it should be played with a light, crisp accent. A staccato note or chord receives less than half its indicated value.

A triangle above or below a note or chord also indicates staccato; usually with somewhat more stress.

Ties

The tie is similar in appearance to the slur. The tie indicates that two notes of the same pitch to be played as one note value.

When two or more ties are used in sequence, the note should be held for the combined value of all tied notes.

Phrase Mark

Like the slur, the *phrase mark* indicates that a passage be played in a smooth and connected manner. Each phrase of a piece is expressed as a distinctive musical idea, like a sentence.

DYNAMICS

Dynamic Marks

ppp	**Pianississimo**	As soft as possible
pp	**Pianissimo**	Very soft
p	**Piano**	Soft
mp	**Mezzo piano**	Moderately soft
mf	**Mezzo forte**	Moderately loud
f	**Forte**	Loud
ff	**Fortissimo**	Very loud
fff	**Fortississimo**	As loud as possible

Crescendo Mark

A gradual increase in volume is indicated by a *crescendo mark*.

Diminuendo Mark

A gradual decrease in volume is indicated by a diminuendo mark.

ORNAMENTS

Grace Notes

A *grace note* is a small note that adjoins a full-sized note. Most grace notes are unaccented, and should be played as quickly as possible just before the natural beat of the note that follows.

An *accented grace note* (or *appoggiatura*) should be played as quickly as possible right on the natural beat of the attached note.

Grace notes may also occur in groups. These are usually unaccented, as shown.

Mordents

The *upper mordent* calls for the quick alternation of the written note with the note above it.

The *lower mordent* calls for the quick alternation of the written note with the note below it.

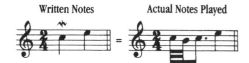

Rolled Chords

A wavy vertical line indicates that a chord should be *rolled*. Chord tones are played one at a time in quick succession, with all notes held for the full duration of the indicated chord.

Tremolo

A tremolo is indicated by two half notes joined together with a beam. These two pitches should each be played twice in an alternating pattern of eighth notes.

Tremolos may also be applied to other note values by adding beam marks, as shown.

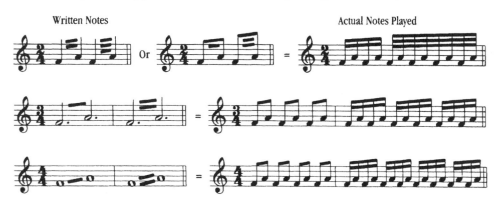

Trill

A *trill* calls for the rapid alternation of a note with the note above it. Long trills often include a wavy line after the trill sign.

TEMPO

Metronome Markings

The metronome is a device that taps out beats at regular intervals. It is used by musicians for setting precise tempos when practicing. Composers may indicate a precise tempo by using a *metronome marking* at the beginning of a piece or section. This indicates the note value of the basic beat and the number of beats per minute for the piece. From left to right, these metronome markings indicate *adagio, moderato, allegro,* and *presto.*

Pieces with time signatures that call for a half note, dotted quarter, or eighth note to equal one beat may include metronome markings with these notes. Each of these metronome markings indicates a moderate tempo (*moderato*).

Fermata

The *fermata sign* (⌢) indicates that a note or chord be held for longer than its full value.

Pause Mark

A *pause mark* (//) indicates that you stop playing briefly before continuing on.

OTHER SYMBOLS

Melody Line

Dotted lines are sometimes used to indicate the movement of the melody line from one hand to another, as shown.

An *octave sign* above the staff indicates that the passage be played an octave higher.

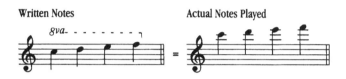

An *octave sign* below the staff indicates that the passage be played an octave lower.

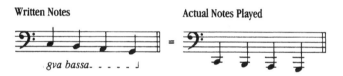

Optional Notes

Small notes (usually in parentheses) indicate *optional notes* which should be played if possible.

Pedal Markings

The right (sustain) pedal is the most commonly used pedal in piano music. The pedal mark (*↑*) indicates that this pedal should be pressed. This marking (*❀*) is often used to indicate that the pedal should be released. Square brackets are also used to indicate when the right pedal is

REPEATS AND ENDINGS

Repeat Sign

Two dots before a double bar form a *repeat sign*. This sign is often used at the end of a piece indicating that the entire piece should be played twice.

If a *repeat sign* occurs in the middle of a piece, return to the beginning and repeat the first section before moving on.

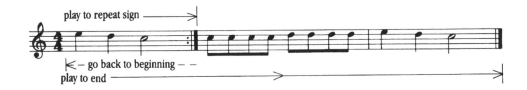

If a mirror image of the repeat sign occurs in a composition, return to this sign when repeating the piece.

Da Capo

D.C. is an abbreviation of the Italian phrase *Da Capo,* meaning "from the head." This marking means the same thing as a single repeat sign—repeat the piece from its beginning.

Dal Segno

D.S. is short for the Italian phrase *Dal Segno,* meaning "from the sign." This marking means you should go back to the *dal segno sign* (𝄋) and repeat the section.

Alternate Endings

Some compositions feature *alternate endings,* each marked with a bracket and numeral. The second time through the piece, you should skip the first ending and play the second ending.

D.C. al Coda

This marking means you should repeat the piece until you reach the *coda sign* (⊕), then skip to the next coda sign and end the piece with the *coda* (meaning "tail").

D.S. al Coda

This marking indicates you should repeat the piece from the *dal segno sign* (𝄋). Once you reach the coda sign, skip to the next coda sign, then play the coda to end the piece.

D.C. al Fine

Fine is the Italian word for "end." This marking is used in conjunction with repeat markings to indicate the point at which the piece ends. *D.C. al Fine* indicates that you should go back to the beginning of the piece and repeat until you come to the marking *Fine.*

D.S. al Fine

D.S. al Fine tells you to go back to the *dal segno* sign and repeat until the point marked *Fine.*

TABLE OF NOTES

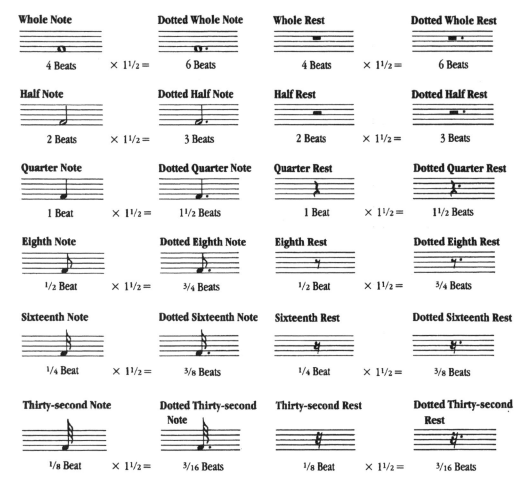

Double-dotted Notes

A note or rest followed by two dots is worth 1¾ its normal value.

Triplets

Three quarter notes form a triplet lasting two beats.

Here three sixteenth notes form a triplet lasting one-half of a beat and three thirty-second notes form a triplet lasting one quarter of a beat.

Here each dotted eighth note lasts one-half of a beat. Each eighth rest lasts one-third of a beat.

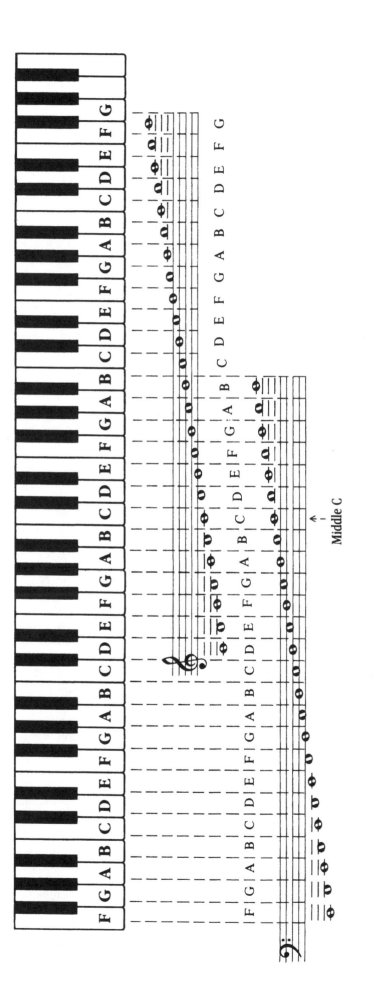

Middle C

GLOSSARY OF MUSIC TERMS

Adagio Slowly.

Adagio cantabile Slowly, in a singing manner.

Adagio e legato Slowly and smoothly.

Adagio sostenuto Slowly and sustained.

Accelerando (abbr. **accel.**) Growing faster.

Allargando (abbr. **allarg.**) Growing slower.

Allegretto Moderately fast.

Allegro Quickly.

Allegro con brio Quickly and spiritedly.

Allegro moderato A quick, but moderate, tempo.

Allegro ma non troppo Quickly, but not too much so.

Andante Moderately slowly; a walking pace.

Andante grazioso Moderately slowly and gracefully.

Andante moderato Slowly, but slightly faster than **Andante.**

Andantino Moderately slowly; a brisk walking pace.

A tempo Return to the previous rate of speed.

Cantabile As if sung.

Coda A passage of music played at the end of a piece. (See "Music Symbols")

Con pedal (abbr. **con ped.**) With pedal; indicates that the right (sustain) pedal is to be pressed as needed. (See "Music Symbols")

Crescendo (abbr. **cresc.**) Growing louder. (See "Music Symbols")

D.C., D.C. al Coda, D.C. al Fine, D.S., D.S. al Coda, D.S. al Fine, (also **D.S. al Fine**) (See "Music Symbols")

Diminuendo (abbr. **dim.**) (also **decrescendo,** abbr. **decresc.**) Growing softer. (See "Music Symbols")

Dolce Sweetly.

Espressivo (abbr. **espress.**) Expressively; with feeling.

Fine The end of a repeated passage or piece. (See "Music Symbols")

Galop A fast dance tune.

Largo Very slow and stately.

Legato Smoothly, with each note lasting its full value.

Lento Slowly.

Moderato Moderately fast.

Pedal (abbr. **ped.** or ℞.) Depress right (sustain) pedal. (See "Music Symbols")

Pedal simile (abbr. **ped. simile** or ℞. **simile**) Pedal as previously marked.

Più forte (abbr. **più** f) Even louder. (See "Music Symbols")

Poco a poco crescendo (abbr. **poco a poco cresc.**) Growing louder little by little.

Poco a poco diminuendo (abbr. **poco a poco dim.**) Growing softer little by little.

Poco crescendo (abbr. **poco cresc.**) Growing a little louder.

Poco diminuendo (abbr. **poco dim.**) Growing a little softer.

Poco ritardando (abbr. **poco rit.** or **poco ritard.**) A little slower.

Presto Rapidly.

Rallentando (abbr. **rall.**) Growing slower and slower.

Ritardando (abbr. **rit.** or **ritard.**) Growing slower.

Ritardando e diminuendo (abbr. **rit. e dim.** or **ritard. e dim.**) Growing slower and softer.

Sempre Always; throughout.

Sempre pp **e senza sordini** Very softly throughout and "without dampers"; *i.e.* with the sustain pedal depressed.

Senza ripetizione Without repeats.

Simile In the same style as before.

Staccato (abbr. **stacc.**) Lightly accented, with each note lasting less than its full value. (See "Music Symbols")

Tempo primo (abbr. **Tempo I**) Return to the tempo used at the beginning of the first section of the piece.

Trio A second dance section in a minuet, waltz, or march, usually followed by a repeat of the first section.